TASHA TUDOR'S DOLLHOUSE

A Lifetime in Miniature

TASHA TUDOR'S DOLLHOUSE

A Lifetime in Miniature

Text by
HARRY DAVIS

Photographs by
JAY PAUL

LITTLE, BROWN AND COMPANY
Boston   New York   London

FIRST EDITION

Library of Congress Cataloging-in-Publication Data
　　Davis, Harry.
　　Tasha Tudor's dollhouse : a lifetime in miniature / text by Harry Davis ;
　　　　photographs by Jay Paul. — 1st ed.
　　　　　　p.　　cm.
　　ISBN 0-316-85521-9
　　1. Dollhouses — United States — History — 20th century.
　　2. Tudor, Tasha — Art collections.　I. Paul, Jay.　II. Title.
　　NK4892.5.T84D38　1999
　　745.592'3'092 — dc21　99-14138

10　9　8　7　6　5　4　3　2　1

RRD-VA

Book design by Melodie Wertelet
House drawing by Mary Reilly, based on original blueprint

Printed in the United States of America

To James Robert Orum

Contents

Introduction

TASHA TUDOR, the renowned author and illustrator of children's books, has in recent years become something of a lifestyle icon. In *The Private World of Tasha Tudor* she attempted to show the unique 1830s world she has recreated as her own. So successful were her efforts that *Tasha Tudor's Cookbook, Tasha Tudor's Garden*, and *Tasha Tudor's Heirloom Crafts* soon followed and gave readers an intimate look into a lifestyle and body of work that, at some point, became almost interchangeable.

From early childhood, she also maintained a miniature version of the highly original life she was living. Beginning with her first dollhouse crafted by her mother for her seventh Christmas, in 1922, Tasha, to this day, maintains an active interest in the parallel life her dollhouse represents.

That first dollhouse must have been extraordinary. Tasha's mother, the renowned portrait painter Rosamond Tudor, was a talented artist in many mediums. Tasha recalls the details, still impressed by the ingenious use of materials. "It was incredible. It was called Pumpkin House because it was supposed to be magic, like Cinderella's pumpkin. The outside of the house was landscaped with bushes made of dyed-green sponges, the lawn was made of green velvet, and wild cranberry vines dipped in wax climbed on the house. It was surrounded by a white picket fence Mamma had made from meat skewers. It was all very effective."

Naturally, over the course of more than seventy-seven years, the details of the dollhouse collection have been altered as time and circumstances dictated. The dolls have changed residences many times; their possessions have been added to and upgraded. The makeup of the doll family itself has changed as one doll or another left the family to go with a grown child, perhaps to start another miniature version of a life all its own, still part of a wonderful extended family of the imagination.

As with many families, a hint of growing pains, mild scandal if you will, exists with the current residents of Tasha's dollhouse. Captain Thaddeus Crane is the man of the house and has been since Tasha first made him nearly half a century ago. Not liking the way most male dolls were made at that time, Tasha was determined to make him masculine. "Most men dolls looked so effeminate, like lady dolls with mustaches pasted on. I modeled his face out of clay, first, and then cast it in plaster of paris, filling the mold with plastic wood that hardens very quickly. His body was made of leather and I carved his hands and feet from wood." Captain Crane became a very manly figure and rather well known. He has appeared in a number of Tasha's book illustrations and was the subject

EMMA and THADDEUS

of a 1955 *LIFE* magazine article when he married Melissa Shakespeare, a doll that had belonged to Tasha's aunt Edith Burgess and was the inspiration for one of Tasha's most beloved books, *A Is for Annabelle*. With such a highly publicized marriage and a rather high-profile literary life, one could imagine that the marriage might not last. It didn't. Decades later, in Tasha's discreet explanation, "Emma came along and there was some trouble."

A friend had enlisted Tasha's aid in making a doll for herself. Tasha decided the easiest way to show her how it was done was to make a doll with her, demonstrating the process. The friend made a successful doll and Tasha made Emma. "It was a case of Pygmalion, I guess. I fell in love with Emma and it changed my feelings for the other dolls. Emma was different from the others and lovely to look at. Thaddeus thought so, too."

Melissa and Captain Crane parted amicably and now the good Captain and Emma Birdwhistle, the most detailed of all of Tasha's dolls, share the dollhouse. In this respect, the 1830s became the 1990s and, like any young, newly married second wife, Emma has made the dollhouse very much her own, reshaped by a great deal of shopping and, in 1996, by the building of an entirely new house to hold the acquisitions of Tasha's lifetime.

It is no secret that Emma is something of an alter ego for Tasha. Emma's interests are Tasha's, and a few rare watercolors signed "E.B." bear a remarkable resemblance to Tasha's own work. Tasha correctly compares their relationship with Pygmalion and Galatea, with herself as the sculptor who fell in love with his own creation.

Tasha doesn't analyze her fascination for small objects that fuels the ongoing creation of the dollhouse. She simply uses it as a means to have fun, to continue to play house, using artistic judgment, collecting skills, and mature resources honed over a full and vibrant lifetime.

The contents of the dollhouse have been gathered over a period spanning nearly eight decades. Furniture and accessories were purchased, traded, and received as gifts. Family members and friends have recreated pieces in miniature, copying originals from Tasha's house, Corgi Cottage, in Vermont. A few pieces were received as fees for lectures or portrait commissions. Their acquisition reflects an abiding interest that weathered all the changing circumstances of a private and professional life, and today they form a remarkable collection that mirrors a remarkable life.

TASHA TUDOR'S DOLLHOUSE

A Lifetime in Miniature

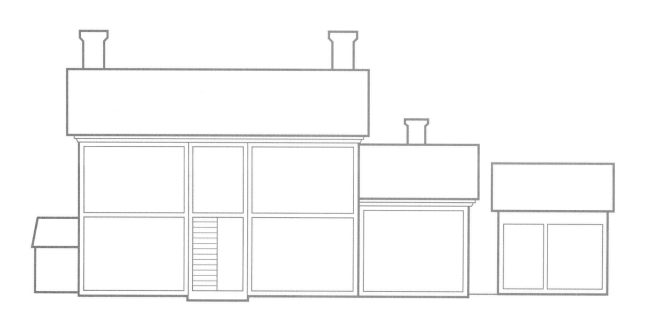

The House

A MASTER TEAM OF ARTISTS from Colonial Williamsburg created Tasha's current dollhouse in 1996. When the Abby Aldrich Rockefeller Folk Art Center in Williamsburg decided to mount an exhibition of Tasha's art and her art of living, the dollhouse was seen as a vital part of the exhibit. The treasures Tasha had collected were a unique collection in their own right, but as a reflection in miniature of her life, they were integral to the spirit of the exhibition.

Since building Corgi Cottage in 1971, Tasha had not had a dollhouse large enough to house the entire collection. She had room settings in built-in cases along a wall adjacent to her bedroom. They could not travel nor were they large enough to hold all of Emma and Thaddeus's possessions. Carolyn Weekly, the director of the folk art center, offered to study the collection and have a house built to display everything in an appropriate setting. Tasha accepted the offer with enthusiasm and they began at once to collaborate on the design.

A team of five artisans worked for five months constructing the dollhouse, amassing a total of 780 working hours in doing so. Sharon Keith, who coordinated the team, was the only miniaturist in the group and the only one with dollhouse experience. The four men were experienced in working with wood but had not worked together before this project, except as guides in an eighteenth-century tools exhibit at Colonial Williamsburg.

The scale was a new experience for Sharon. Most dollhouses are scaled one inch to one foot. Tasha's is one-fourth human size. "I had worked on half-inch or one-inch dollhouse scale but nothing this large. The most fun was coordinating all these men who talked about their shops, their machinery, and their tools. My drill press is six inches tall and my table saw is four inches square, so I couldn't do any of the actual cutting. In the smaller scales, you can find everything ready-made, but in this scale, everybody had to manufacture everything. There were no windows or doors that size, no roofing material, no paneling. Everything had to be done from scratch."

The other members of the team were Dean Couch, Bob Cookingham, Roger Cunningham, and Bill Kafes. They were given a minimal line drawing of the house and relatively free rein as to the details. They began work on a totally custom-made piece knowing it would test their individual problem-solving skills. They soon realized that a major collaborative effort was taking place.

They each had individual responsibilities. On the house proper, Roger Cunningham did doors, windows, crown molding, and baseboards; Bill Kafes did flooring and chimneys; Bob Cookingham did roofs; Dean Couch did exterior siding, paneling, and the fireplace; and Sharon, in addition to coordinating and securing materials, did the fireplace hearth and the painting of the chimneys. After fabricating the materials, they divided the assembly and installation of the rooms among themselves.

Dean Couch built the center hall completely, and shared construction of the greenhouse with Sharon, who did the masonry work and the brick floor. He also volunteered to build the goat barn with assistance from Bob and Roger. The details and complexity of the construction are impressive as was the crew's enthusiasm for the project. The team met with Tasha several times during the construction but her most repeated advice was to "just have fun with it."

The finished project was to be a simple, straightforward Victorian farmhouse. "Since the original design was pretty general," remembers Roger, "we worked out a lot of the details ourselves." Sharon is proud that "a lot of tech-

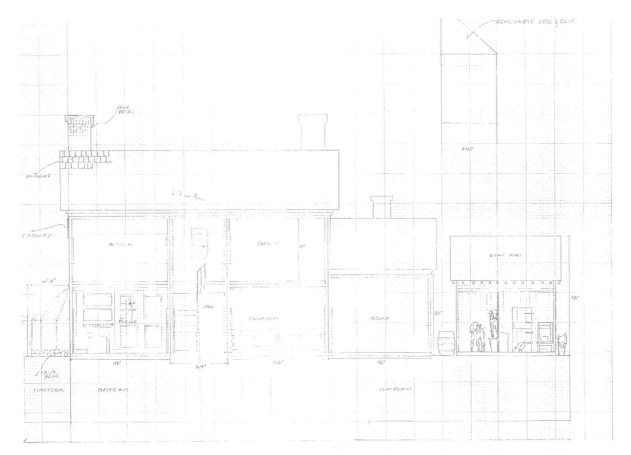

The working BLUEPRINT for the dollhouse, though sketchy, provided the builders with the basic plan.

The craftspeople who built the **DOLLHOUSE** worked from a simple original plan, but did extensive research as they developed the details. Dean Couch constructed the greenhouse in his home workshop after measuring and photographing Tasha's own in Vermont. Tasha supplied Dean with sketches of the goat barn, including the "goat cafeteria" and the milking stand. Final assembly of the dollhouse took place in the gallery of the Abby Aldrich Rockefeller Folk Art Center in Williamsburg in the weeks prior to the opening of the landmark exhibition, on November 2, 1996. Dramatically lit, the dollhouse was the focal point of the show. Plexiglas covered the front of the rooms and allowed visitors to observe them up close.

niques just evolved as we went along." She used a thin coat of plaster to form the bricks in the greenhouse floor, scoring it rapidly before it dried, to simulate individual bricks. After painting the entire floor a background color, she painted each separate brick using several colors.

According to Roger, "it wasn't daunting because we all had something to contribute." The team developed a sense of camaraderie as the work progressed. Bob Cookingham considered it "a true collaborative effort. As soon as I finished the roof sections, I came over and worked with Dean in his shop, and Bill and I discussed the making of his chimneys."

A great deal of thought went into each stage, and this aspect impressed Bill Kafes. "You don't realize until you attempt to do something how much intellectual work goes into what may appear to be a relatively simple project. The intellectual work, in some ways, takes as much time as doing the work itself."

The thought behind each part of the construction is evident. The doors presented a special challenge to Roger. "We wanted to show the image of a panel on a solid door. I made a template and routed it out about one thirty-second of an inch, and you could see the difference. The downstairs doors have panels put in the middle of them to make them fancy doors, and the everyday doors are upstairs."

The goat barn is a masterpiece in miniature. The appearance and mood effectively capture the feel of Tasha's own barn. The attention to detail is extraordinary. Tasha made a few sketches for Dean, concentrating on the practical needs of a working barn, including the milking stand and the feeding compartments. Dean studied Tasha's books *The Private World* and *Heirloom Crafts* for extra details such as the long rectangular windows, made by Roger.

"I didn't know how to scale the milking stand. In looking at a photograph in the book, I realized there was a pair of scissors hanging on the wall. From looking at them, I estimated they were eight inches long, so I made my own scale with eight inches as my master and I used that to scale the milking stand down.

"From looking at how her barn was built, I used post-and-beam construction, which is how, I guess, all barns are built. I built it just like the Amish build a barn. You make a frame for the ends and then you bring them up and you make the back frame. It worked out fine."

Although Dean built the major portion of the barn, including two Dutch doors, he's quick to share credit. "Bob made the roof and helped assemble the siding. He made the hayloft ladder and the working pulley outside the door. Roger made the windows."

Tasha gave the barn its greatest compliment. She first saw the completed dollhouse at a small gathering before the exhibit opened. When she reached the barn, she turned to Dean and said, "It makes me homesick."

Extended members of the team added their efforts to the house. The Colonial Williamsburg paint department did all the painting and staining, and, once the house was assembled, their electricians did the wiring. Because the finished house was so large, seven and a half feet tall and nineteen feet long, no one had seen it completely fitted together. The team was anxious to know for sure that everything connected properly. When it was assembled in the gallery, each piece fit superbly, and there was a collective sigh of relief and satisfaction from the proud artisans. Dean recalls, "To a person, I think we were kind of sad when it was finished. It was so much fun doing it."

The afternoon before the exhibit opened, on November 2, 1996, Tasha was busy putting finishing touches on the arrangements before the fronts were sealed with protective Plexiglas. A few of Emma's things in her bedroom were repositioned and minor changes to the kitchen were made. Tasha's final addition was to the goat barn, where she scattered peppercorns to simulate goat droppings, making the barn and the dollhouse accurate down to the last detail.

The entire exhibition, "Take Joy! The World of Tasha Tudor," was a major success. Attendance at the six-month show was higher than for any previous exhibition the museum had hosted. The dollhouse was the most popular display. It combined all the aspects of Tasha's world and presented it in both an imaginative and practical way. Viewing the house does give a real look into what life at Corgi Cottage is like. A great many of the things Tasha surrounds herself with at home are here. It is quite possible to feel what Tasha's days are like by examining the surroundings of the dolls.

Tasha was delighted with the results of many months of consultation, planning, and construction. The dollhouse was an ideal showcase for a lifetime of collecting, and the perfect home for Emma and Thaddeus. Tasha was somewhat dismayed at the scope the collection had taken on. Even the scale of the large museum galleries did little to conceal the size of the dollhouse. It would have to remain in Virginia for exhibition purposes; its size wouldn't permit its display at Corgi Cottage. Tasha was content for it to do so. It had taken on a life of its own, which was Tasha's ultimate goal for her miniature version of the world. It had a vibrancy not unlike its full-size counterpart, Corgi Cottage.

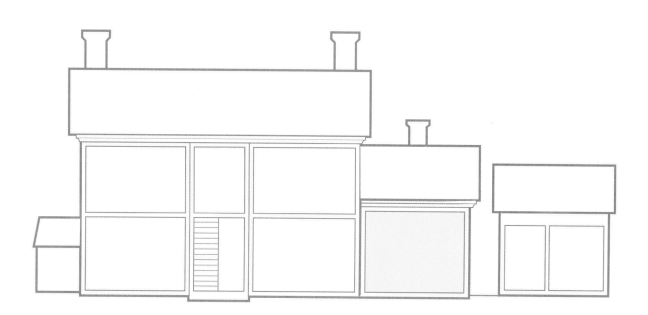

The Kitchen

NO ROOM IN THE DOLLHOUSE is more like the corresponding room in Tasha's own house in spirit and detail than the kitchen. The kitchen has always been Tasha's favorite room in any dollhouse she has ever had. That first dollhouse, created for her by her mother as a Christmas present when Tasha was seven, was inadequate as far as its kitchen was concerned, and Tasha immediately rectified the situation. "The kitchen was way in the back, behind two little doors. You could hardly get into it. Mamma didn't like to cook, you see. The dining room, in front of the kitchen, was much larger. I took the little doors down and did away with the dining room. I made the whole room into a big kitchen."

Today, at Corgi Cottage, the kitchen is the center of all activity, and the dollhouse kitchen reflects that. Tasha's own kitchen boasts a great collection of antique cooking implements of every description: copper pots, cobalt-blue-decorated pottery, baskets, yellowware mixing bowls, and wooden and tin tools for almost every aspect of food

Emma's **TIN KITCHEN**, an exact replica of Tasha's own, stands ready to prepare Christmas dinner. When placed in front of the fireplace, the tin kitchen becomes a reflector oven and perfectly roasts the fowl held in place by a rotating spit.

preparation. In the dollhouse she has managed to replicate her own kitchen in miniature to an amazing degree.

A dominant feature of Tasha's kitchen is the large cast-iron wood-burning stove, which provides welcome heat for the house in winter as well as a slow, even cooking surface and oven. Emma's kitchen is equally impressive with an original miniature cast-iron stove from the 1830s. So perfectly reproduced that it can actually be used, Tasha

Emma's **CAST-IRON STOVE**, either a toy or a salesman's sample of a "Little Fanny" model of the 1830s, is completely usable. It can be fed tiny logs and must be tended carefully.

Bright sunlight and a pleasant view make working at
the **SINK** enjoyable, whether it be Emma's or Tasha's.
A miniature masher is ready to mash potatoes, to which
Emma will add cream cheese according to the recipe in
Tasha Tudor's Cookbook.

The kitchen sink is an accurate replica of Tasha's, complete with a working HAND PUMP.

found it years ago at an antique show. The scale was perfect and it became the center-piece for the kitchen in miniature. "The children used to take the stove out and put it on the hearth and cook bacon for the cat. You could put little sticks in it and it would really cook."

Another item in the kitchen that identifies itself as Tasha Tudor's is the kitchen sink. A beautiful copy of Tasha's own, the detail is extraordinary, with a copper basin for water, and a working drain. The copper hand pump, a close copy of Tasha's own, works by virtue of a water-filled olive-oil can beneath the drain. It was made by Tasha's brother-in-law, Lauren McCready. "He copied my pump here and my children loved it because it actually worked."

The **RED CUPBOARD** in the kitchen is a close approximation of Tasha's, as are the arrangement of cobalt-blue-decorated stoneware and the blue-banded cookie jar.

Emma's **COPPER DUSTPAN**, lined with tin, was a gift from Thaddeus, and is appropriately and thoughtfully inscribed.

The working sink and cookstove help one ease into the gentle make-believe of the dollhouse kitchen. Canisters are filled with flour and spices, and every conceivable kitchen tool awaits use. Some of the copper pots are miniatures of the ones Tasha uses every day. A basket of small sticks stands beside the stove, ready for use. It is difficult for the eye to take in so much detail all at once, but the comparison between Tasha's full-size kitchen and the one in the dollhouse helps one understand that, indeed, this is truly a working kitchen.

The stoneware pottery is as varied and detailed as Tasha's originals. A wide range of churns, each with its own tiny dasher, could be used to make butter, whereas storage containers keep things fresh in an 1830s style. Pitchers and jugs abound and all show

Supplies for a SUMMER PICNIC include fresh
vegetables and fruit and an ample basket holding
Thaddeus's favorite champagne.

Thaddeus's **BOTTLES OF MALAGA**, a Spanish dessert wine, are used for cooking. In addition, the dollhouse boasts some excellent champagnes. One bottle always resides on a silver tray on the Shaker candlestand in the dining room. Another may be seen tucked into a picnic basket in the kitchen, awaiting a summer outing.

a remarkable skill in working on a small scale. Many of the copies of Tasha's own pottery were made for her as gifts by friends or admirers who, in many cases, were professional potters. They bear artistic tribute to the willingness of so many to join in the fun of a world in miniature.

A recent addition to Tasha's own collection was a unique wooden dustpan from the late nineteenth century. She found it very pleasing and made much of it while finding the perfect place to hang it. Her son Seth made a miniature copy for her as a Christmas present the following year, as he often has done when his mother has acquired a new favorite.

A variety of **SEASONINGS AND SPICES** are ready to be used when called for by recipes from *Tasha Tudor's Cookbook*.

Things are arranged in the cupboard and on the shelves in the same spirit as Tasha's kitchen. Hundreds of items are where they would be in the real kitchen: cookie cutters, butter molds, rolling pins, dustpans, hot pads, funnels, and graters, molds, plates, tea kettles, mixing bowls, potato mashers, choppers, strainers, and a rack on which to dry dishes after they are washed. Not only is this a real kitchen, but also it is one belonging to an enthusiastic, serious cook.

Many of the pieces are extremely rare. An early pewter porringer shows the same wear a baby of the late eighteenth century would have given it. Tiny ladles and butter molds and bone-handled knives and forks all echo the passing of a century or more in the imaginative world of children learning adult skills and customs by playing with miniature versions of adult tools and implements.

The blue-banded blown-glass **COOKIE JAR** is always filled with cookies, as are the ones in Tasha's kitchen.

One of the most delicate items in the kitchen is a blown-glass storage jar with blue decorative bands. It is a copy of an antique jar that descended in Tasha's family. She located an elderly glassblower known only as Mr. Whittemore, who agreed to make a miniature copy of her original. It is exquisite and remains filled with real cookies made from Tasha's own recipes, just as Tasha's original jar does. The skill needed to produce such pieces is as extraordinary as the joy with which Tasha has pursued their reproduction. She has followed every lead or recommendation about a skilled craftsperson. In the tradition of early dollhouses, the pieces are often recreated by an artisan who normally works in regular scale. The task of working in miniature becomes more arduous as a result, but the finished piece is authentic, and that aspect is most important to Tasha.

The Dining Room

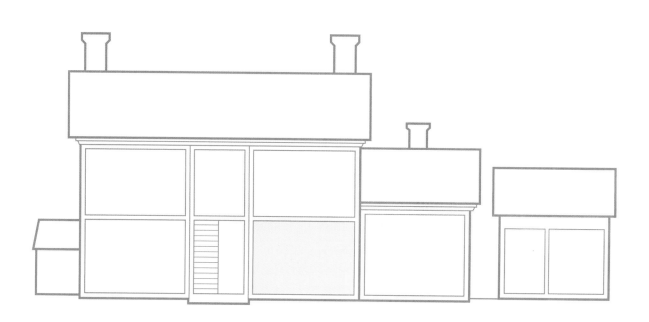

The Dining Room

THERE IS AN AIR OF INFORMALITY about the dollhouse's dining room, even though it is a formal room. Stacks of china bear witness to Emma and Thaddeus's love of entertaining, and Tasha has repeated in miniature her own stacks of blue-and-white china, these in a transfer floral pattern that she finds eminently satisfying. Consisting of forty pieces, the service is complete with both dinner and luncheon plates, bowls, platters, covered dishes, a gravy boat, and a soup tureen. An early japanned mirror hangs over a grained Empire sideboard bountiful with antique silver baskets and bottles of wine. A Shaker candlestand boasts a silver tray and a particularly fine bottle of champagne. This is clearly a room in which eating and drinking are meant to be enjoyed.

An impressive feature of the dining room is its oriental rug, of southwest Persian origin, which gives warmth and color to the room. The intricacy of its geometric pattern is rare in a rug so small.

The **DINING-ROOM TABLE** is set for a small dinner party using part of the blue-and-white transfer dinner service. A pewter pepper pot and master salt are permanent fixtures here. The tiny salt spoon is indicative of a master pewtersmith's skill and patience.

The **JAPANNED MIRROR** over the sideboard has wonderfully aged and diffused glass.

The glassblower who crafted the blue-banded cookie jar in the kitchen also made the handblown **WINE GLASSES**.

Matching plates with hand-painted flowers flank the shelf containing a set of red wine glasses hand-blown by the same Mr. Whittemore who crafted Tasha's blue-banded storage jar in the kitchen.

A tall chest of drawers holds additional silver, linens, and china, making this room well equipped for entertaining.

The Parlor

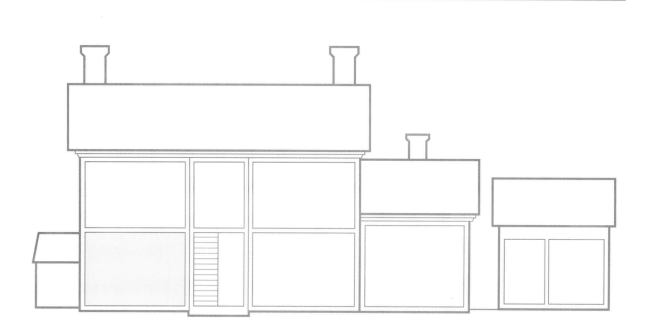

The Parlor

ASHA'S PARLOR AT CORGI COTTAGE is attractively formal and seldom used. Tasha spends most of her time in the winter kitchen, reserving the parlor for special occasions: a birthday dinner, a celebratory tea, or the unveiling of the Christmas tree. It is the same in the dollhouse. Emma and Thaddeus are most often found in the kitchen or the library. When they do have tea in the parlor, it is as special an event as tea in the life-size parlor at Corgi Cottage.

The fireplace and the paneling in the dollhouse parlor are similar to Tasha's own. The paintings hanging there reflect the art Tasha hangs in the large version. Many of the furnishings are similar, some are exact. The musket hanging over the fireplace is a replica of one owned by Tasha's great-great-grandfather, Col. William Tudor, the first Judge Advocate General of the United States under George Washington. The original hangs over the mantelpiece in Tasha's winter kitchen.

When Thaddeus's card-playing friends fill the library,
EMMA ENJOYS A BOOK in the silence of the parlor.

TINTYPES and carte de visite photographs of family
and friends fill three photo albums in the library.

A favorite red banister-back chair is a copy of one of Tasha's favorites. It and several others were made by Tasha's daughter-in-law Marjorie Tudor, a talented artist in her own right. The chairs are lathe turned to a degree of delicacy seldom seen. The antique finish and the woven rush seats are faithful to the originals and help make the chairs museum-quality reproductions. Crafted with an extraordinary eye for detail, each chair lists to one side as does the original, and wear and patina are replicated where they appear on the larger version.

A tintype of a younger Thaddeus rests on
a book in the parlor. The **BIRD IN THE
GILDED CAGE** flaps his wings and sings
when wound by a key in the shape of a bird.
It is similar to the bird in Tasha's own parlor.

One treasure in Tasha's parlor is a gilded birdcage, which is home to a feathered
mechanical bird who turns on his perch and flaps his wings as he sings. Tasha shows
the bird to special guests, and his performance is both a privilege and a surprisingly
good musical presentation.

The dollhouse parlor contains a miniature version of the performing bird in his
gilded cage. He is wound by a tiny key in the shape of a bird. The filigree work on the
cage is jewel-like in its detail, and the tiny bird and his song duplicate the artistry of
the original.

The dollhouse has three complete TEA SETS. This one is Emma's favorite and the one most often used. The cookies were made from one of Tasha's recipes.

Tea is laid out much the same way in the dollhouse as at Tasha's tea table; properly, of course, but informally, with the pleasure of the ceremony being uppermost. Fresh flowers are a necessity and the parlor boasts an oft-used, handsome, rose-medallion vase, among others. The tilt-top tea table was made by the eminent yacht designer Nathanael Herreshoff, who also designed Emma and Thaddeus's bed. Mr. Herreshoff was a colleague of Tasha's father, William Starling Burgess, who himself was quite well known as a naval architect, having designed three successful America's Cup defenders. Candlelight is important to the parlor as well as to the other rooms of the dollhouse, and although there are electricity and electric lamps, they are used as sparingly in the dollhouse as they are in Tasha's home.

AFTERNOON TEA in the parlor is a daily ritual in the dollhouse. Naturally, Tasha Tudor's Welsh Breakfast Tea is preferred. Tasha worked for more than a year to perfect the blend of her own brand of tea, which she sells through her company, Corgi Cottage Industries. The dollhouse kitchen always has a full canister of the distinctive blend.

The delicacy of the crystal **CHANDELIER** is a tribute to gifted artisans at Corning Glass Works. Several versions were created until Tasha pronounced this one perfect.

The main source of lighting in the parlor is an extraordinary crystal chandelier that hangs from the ceiling and is perfectly proportioned for the room. Fans of Tasha's at Corning Glass Works created it. The execution was a combined effort, with Tasha first making a model in clay to ensure that the proportions were correct. It produces a soft light that makes the room cozy and inviting.

One of the more recent additions to the parlor shows both Tasha's resourcefulness and the extent to which she can enlist the aid of others to join in her commitment to this small version of her world. The fireplace was always a focal point of the room with its brass fender and andirons supporting miniature logs. It became more of a focal point with the addition of a polar-bear rug in front of it. The rug came with a price. Several winters ago, an ermine got into Tasha's henhouse and created devastation, slaughtering ten of Tasha's prized hens and, on a second visit, Tasha's favorite

The **POLAR-BEAR RUG** epitomizes Tasha's resourcefulness and sense of fair play.

rooster. He had to be stopped, and Tasha and her grandson, Winslow, captured and shot the marauding villain. Mindful of his cruel beauty and his need to pay for his deeds, Tasha decided he would make a perfect polar-bear rug. A taxidermist, recommended by friends, agreed to make the transformation, and the new rug appeared midway through the exhibition at Colonial Williamsburg. The saga of the rug demonstrates again how the dollhouse reflects the actual events of Tasha's own life. It isn't a static display version of a house. It is a portrait of a life presented in miniature. Little is wasted in Tasha's real life, and she extends that same philosophy to the dollhouse.

The working tall-case clock in the parlor is similar to one Tasha keeps in the kitchen at Corgi Cottage. The gentle ticking is more important than the accuracy of the time it keeps, since the Cottage runs on its own timeless rhythms.

The Greenhouse

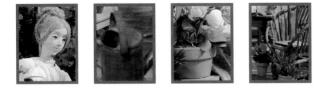 # The Greenhouse

TASHA'S GREENHOUSE is connected to the rest of the house by a long corridor reached by a flight of stairs descending just off the parlor. The connection allows her to move about freely in winter without having to go outside. The dollhouse greenhouse affords Emma and Thaddeus the same opportunity.

Tasha's greenhouse serves two important functions: it protects delicate plants that could not survive the winter outside, and it provides her with continuously blooming flowers, which produce a colorful contrast to the cold snowscapes that surround Corgi Cottage for a predictable portion of each year.

Emma's greenhouse gives that same lush, near-tropical feel to the dollhouse. It is vibrant with color. Potted plants are everywhere and a lavish display of ivy, having outgrown its trellis, extends around the doorway and trails down the side of the wall.

The greenhouse provides **FRESH FLOWERS**
year-round as well as a place to visit spring during
the winter. Both Tasha and Emma pass enjoyable
hours in their greenhouses each day.

EMMA, LIKE TASHA, often can be found
in a contemplative mood in the greenhouse.

Weathered furniture competes for space with a variety of extra terra-cotta pots in
many shapes and sizes. Some of them are antique, acquired by Tasha in England at the
same time she found the larger ones that fill her own potting shed. Stacked around the
brick floor, they provide a feel of imminent activity. An iron cauldron in one corner du-
plicates the one in Tasha's greenhouse, which provides a winter home to the goldfish
that otherwise live in the small pond visible from Tasha's bedroom.

The **GREENHOUSE** is a close replica of
Tasha's own. In the full-size version, one
enters the door through Tasha's herb garden.

Outside, the stone walls supporting the tall glass panels of the greenhouse are close

copies of the originals, as are the windows facing east and the weathered door.

The whole effect of the greenhouse is that of a miniature world within a miniature

world, and the result is mesmerizing.

The Center Hall

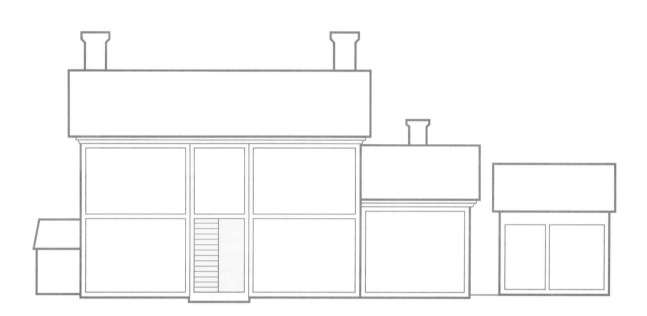

The Center Hall

THE MAIN PURPOSE of the center hall is to provide access to the upstairs. Consequently, its furnishings are sparse. A round, braided rug covers the floor, one of many such rugs used throughout the house. The miniature patterns look exactly like their full-size counterparts, although their construction is much more intricate. Many of them are made of dyed silk stockings, and each one lends an authentic air to its room.

An impressive brass sconce provides light to the hall, and one of Marjorie Tudor's miniature chairs reproduces accurately one of Tasha's banister-back chairs. The original of this one was found by Tasha's old friend Roger Bacon, a well-known New England antiques dealer who shared Tasha's passion for early furniture.

The centerpiece of the hall is a fine display cabinet housing a collection of tiny mementos of Tasha's travels and showcasing her admiration for fellow artist Beatrix Potter. Miniature bronze animals fill the case. Many are Austrian bronzes with expressive

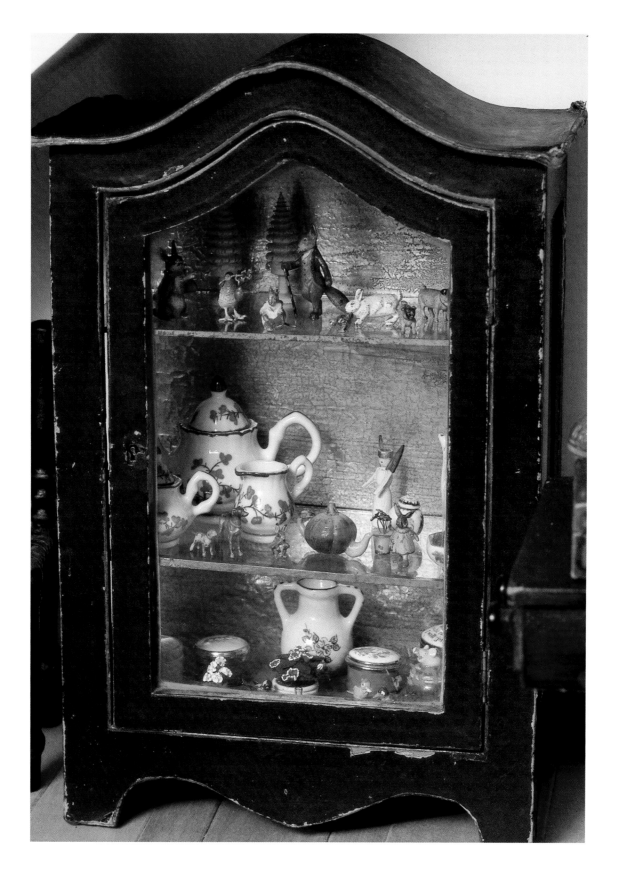

The pride of the curio cabinet are several Austrian
bronze **FIGURINES**, some of which portray Beatrix
Potter characters.

faces and detailed clothing. A proud fox wearing a red waistcoat and carrying a cane,

an exquisite bird holding in its beak a branch bearing a single berry, an owl, pug dogs,

a white rabbit, a lady rabbit wearing a blue apron and red shoes, a pot of flowers, and

a variety of birds form an impressive collection. Benjamin Bunny and Hunca Munca

mouse were gifts from Leslie Linder, the enthusiastic chronicler of the history and

works of Beatrix Potter.

Marjorie Tudor, Tasha's daughter-in-law, carefully crafted the chair, a copy of Tasha's own,
to provide seating in the CENTER HALL.
The English brass girandole, or ornamental
branched candlestick, is an especially fine piece.

Without Mr. Linder's book, *The History of the Writings of Beatrix Potter*, much of
Miss Potter's work would have remained undiscovered. Tasha got to know him and
his sister well during a stay in England in the late 1950s. He was quite taken with
Tasha's doll family and presented the bronzes to her for her dollhouse. He and the
dolls corresponded over the years, sometimes in Beatrix Potter's code, which he had
deciphered.

The miniature-bronzes collection is an excellent example of a unique aspect of
Tasha's dollhouse. Within the large collection are smaller collections of the same
makeup that any household might have, things gathered in travels, items focusing on
an area of special interest, Victorian-style knickknacks. Emma and Thaddeus have
possessions just like all of us, gathered over a lifetime of changing interests and for-
tunes. It is the richness and diversity of their lives in miniature that make them so
interesting and lifelike and that convey a sense of their actually living in Tasha's
dollhouse.

The Bedroom

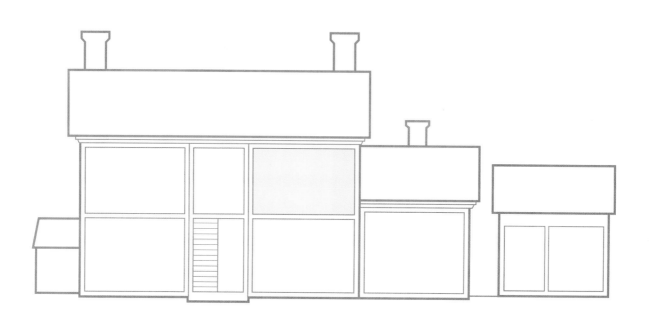

 # The Bedroom

EMMA AND THADDEUS'S BEDROOM contains an elegantly simple, canopied four-poster made by Nathanael Herreshoff, the famous naval architect. The bed linens are very similar to Tasha's own. Linen sheets cover the feather mattress, which is supported by ropes in the appropriate 1830s style. Linen pillowcases and a bolster cover protect down-filled pillows. A much-used antique quilt covers the bed.

One of Marjorie Tudor's chairs, copied from a chair at Corgi Cottage, provides seating. Storage is the main necessity in this room. A towering highboy of simple lines and imposing brasses provides the most accessible space for the extensive wardrobes of both dolls. Boxes filled with jewelry attest to inheritances from earlier family dolls. Some of the drawers are full of Emma's accessories, including fans, purses, and slippers.

A superbly constructed walnut blanket chest with its original key holds infrequently used items. The overflow of accessories fills leather trunks, wallpaper band boxes, and a profusion of other boxes and baskets.

Wearing a dress of homespun cotton, EMMA PREPARES
FOR THE DAY by brushing her hair. Her necessaire contains a complete set of hairbrushes, a clothes brush, and a
toothbrush.

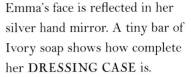

Emma's face is reflected in her silver hand mirror. A tiny bar of Ivory soap shows how complete her **DRESSING CASE** is.

Both Emma and Thaddeus have all the necessities for grooming and dressing. They each have leather necessaires, or toiletry cases, that contain mirrors, combs, hairbrushes, toothbrushes, soap, buttonhooks, shoehorns, and odd storage jars. Thaddeus's case has a usable safety razor with extra blades. Emma's contains a number of cosmetics, including glass vials of perfume inscribed "Emma." Thaddeus prefers a French cologne and currently has a nearly full bottle.

Tasha masterfully designed and sewed each piece of Emma's clothing, which is authentic to the 1830s, the detail being identical to that found in full-size clothing of the

DRIED FLOWERS
from Tasha's garden form
a Valentine bouquet.

period. In that sense, Emma's wardrobe is similar in authenticity to that of a fashion doll. Her clothing is divided between formal gowns and at-home dresses suitable for the domestic life so apparent throughout the dollhouse. A flowing cape adds a dramatic flair to her wardrobe and a tiny "pocket," the kind worn under a lady's dress in the 1830s as a forerunner of today's purse, adds another authentic detail of life in, and the fashion of, the period.

A wire dressmaker's model stands ready should Emma require a new dress. She usually wears an appliquéd skirt, worn with an extremely delicate lace blouse copied from one in Tasha's clothing collection.

The dollhouse bedroom contains a finely crafted
bed fitted with antique linens. The **HIGHBOY**
and the **BLANKET CHEST** at the foot of the
bed hold clothes and accessories. Marjorie Tudor
made the chair, a reproduction of one of Tasha's.

Thaddeus's daily dress is a natural linen three-piece suit with a high-collared cotton shirt. A Union soldier's uniform, complete with greatcoat, was diplomatically put away when he traveled with the dollhouse collection to Colonial Williamsburg for the exhibit at the folk art center. More useful there were his formal swallowtail coat, trousers, and vest.

A Waterbury carriage clock records the time, and the requisite braided rugs add warmth to the comfortable clutter of the bedroom. A painted and worn washstand holds a wash bowl and pitcher, and several chamber pots are tucked discreetly into corners or underneath the bedskirt.

A small portrait of Emma painted in Paris and sent as a Christmas present to Tasha by a friend hangs next to the highboy. A period petipoint floral tapestry and a tiny cross-stitch sampler add decorative accents to the walls, as does a small round mirror. All contribute to the feel of comfort, accented by a lifetime's accumulation of necessities for daily life.

At **BEDTIME**, Emma wears an old
nightshirt belonging to Thaddeus.

The Library

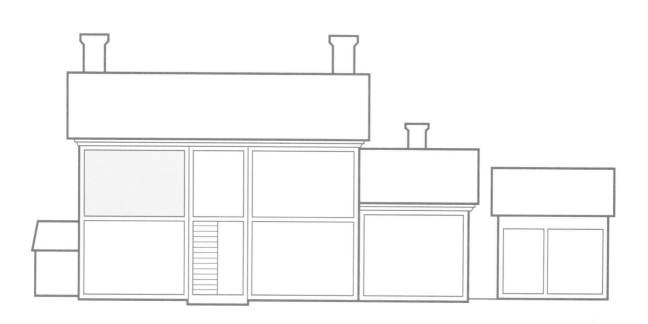

 # The Library

THE LIBRARY IS A PLEASANT, versatile room where a variety of activities take place. Emma's spinning wheel and wool winder reflect Tasha's love of spinning and weaving and of being industrious in the winter when outside activities are kept to a minimum.

Games provide amusement here, and a chess set, dominoes, and cards ensure communal activity around a candlelit table well supplied with refreshments and the pleasures of the pipe. A collection of musical instruments is varied enough to outfit a small orchestra, and, in fact, it does. When one of Tasha's marionette shows is performed, Thaddeus's instruments, including a violin, cello, bass, flute, cornet, and trumpet, are loaned to the Corgi Orchestra, under the direction of Corgiville's famous conductor, Pasquelle Felini. The instruments were made by the well-known miniaturist Harry Smith for Tasha's first marionette show, *The Bremen Town Musicians*. They have been used in all productions since and are precisely detailed little instruments.

CHESS, DOMINOES, AND CARDS are all good choices for an evening's entertainment.

A miniature bookstand, a copy of the one Tasha uses on her art table, is available for Emma to paint on. Occasionally a miniature watercolor will appear, signed "E.B.," for Emma Birdwhistle. Amazingly alike in style and execution to the art of Tasha Tudor, the paintings are sometimes presented to friends' dolls as Christmas gifts.

As one might expect in a full-size library, correspondence is taken care of here, and boxes of stationery and envelopes, a writing portfolio, and several inkwells are on hand. Thaddeus seals his envelopes with hot wax imprinted with his own personal emblem before sending off his letters by Tasha's Sparrow Post. This postal system was created when Tasha's children were small, for the purpose of allowing the children and their dolls and animal families to receive letters and surprises meant only for them. A great deal of mail was received and sent via this efficient system. Emma's seal is an heirloom, a bird carved into a piece of carnelian, which formerly belonged to Tasha's aunt Edith Burgess.

All Tasha's dolls have kept up voluminous correspondence with one another and with the dolls of friends for many decades. Letters and seasonal cards are exchanged and carefully preserved. The penmanship is exquisitely minute and the contents are topical. They chronicle more than half a century of family activity. When Tasha's children were small, the firm of Mouse Mills sent out seasonal catalogues from which

Emma displays her **WATERCOLOR** of a small bird, remarkably similar to the style of Tasha Tudor, signed "E.B." The bookstand on which it is displayed is a copy of the one Tasha uses on her own art table.

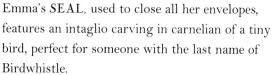

WRITING LETTERS to dolls and children who correspond with Emma and Thaddeus is a favorite pastime. Both dolls have their own stationery and seals. Several inkwells and other writing supplies [opposite] make corresponding easy.

Emma's **SEAL**, used to close all her envelopes, features an intaglio carving in carnelian of a tiny bird, perfect for someone with the last name of Birdwhistle.

the children could order, using buttons for payment. They sent a great many letters ordering clothing for dolls and bears as well as small toys, all of which were supplied to Mouse Mills by Tasha. Other letters recorded the interests and pursuits of the children and their toys as they grew up in a marvelously creative world, half real, half fantasy.

The main focus of the library is, of course, books. The collection includes more than 150 volumes and is as rich and varied as is Tasha's own library.

All of the **BOOKS** in the dollhouse library show evidence
of wear along with the normal signs of aging. They have
been read repeatedly, and favorite quotes from them are
recorded in Emma's commonplace book, a collection of
thoughts that have attracted her attention.

A stack of **SHAKER BOXES** forms a backdrop for Thaddeus's **BRONZE INKWELL** from England.

A wide range of authors, including Cervantes, Dante, Daniel Defoe, and Washington Irving, is represented here, as well as a number of volumes of Shakespeare. Books of poetry and religion abound, as do popular children's fiction and morality stories of the nineteenth century from authors as diverse as "Aunt Laura" and Kate Greenaway.

Leatherbound editions include *Alice in Wonderland, Through the Looking Glass,* and *The History of Little Goody Two-Shoes.* Impressively bound volumes on heraldry and presidents are part of the collection, including one signed by Gerald Ford. A tiny copy of *The Night Before Christmas* reminds us of Tasha's fondness for this poem, which she has illustrated three times. Several albums of tintype photographs, one only of dolls, help to make this library a very personal one for the dolls who live here. Not only do they currently inhabit this house, but also the history of their lives is here, including a journal of their travels and a scrapbook filled with real Victorian scraps, doll-size

In winter, Emma's SPINNING WHEEL is brought into
the library and put to long hours of use. Harry Smith,
a former model maker for the Metropolitan Museum in
New York, meticulously crafted the spinning wheel.

pictures of flowers, animals, birds, and children at play. An original watercolor of "The
Old Woman in the Shoe" provides an engaging frontispiece.

One of the most interesting books in the library is Emma's commonplace book.
A commonplace book was an essential part of many an educated person's personal library in the seventeenth, eighteenth, and early nineteenth centuries. It was a book of
blank pages for jotting down passages from a favorite book or quotations the writer
thought worth remembering. William Byrd and Thomas Jefferson kept commonplace
books. Tasha keeps one and often quotes her favorite writers, especially when one has
succinctly echoed her feelings on a given subject.

Emma's commonplace book, in the tiniest handwriting imaginable, is bound
between cloth covers and contains more than 125 quotes from authors, poets, and
philosophers as varied as William Blake, Sir Walter Raleigh, Mother Goose, George
Bernard Shaw, Thoreau, Oscar Wilde, and Emily Dickinson.

This commonplace book of favorite quotes is another example of the detail that
makes Tasha Tudor's dollhouse appealing. The house was assembled with definite pref-
erences in mind. It consists not of what was found or available but of what was desired,
what was necessary to provide a life in miniature for dolls with distinct personalities
and passionate interests. This gives the house the feeling that it is lived in by highly
original people who happen to be dolls.

The Goat Barn

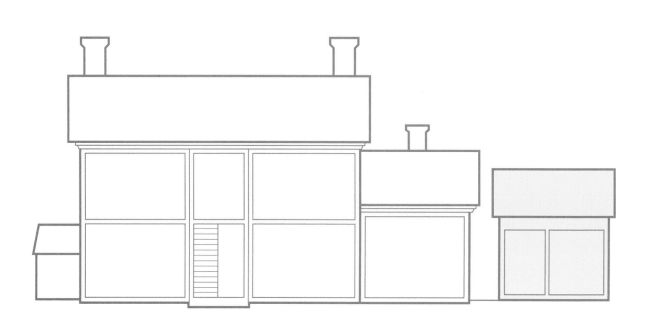

The Goat Barn

THE GOAT BARN is an important part of Corgi Cottage. It houses Tasha's herd of prized silver Nubian goats and is a hub of life and activity. The goats are fed and watered morning and evening, and whichever goats are "fresh" are milked at the same time. Their milk is an integral part of the pantry at Corgi Cottage, often providing butter, cheese, and, in the summer, ice cream.

It was imperative that the dollhouse have a goat barn, and a great deal of care and attention to detail went into the creation of the miniature version, ensuring that it be authentic to the original. The post-and-beam construction follows the craftsmanlike form of Tasha's own barn, built using only hand tools by her son Seth.

The loft does double duty as storage for hay for the long Vermont winter and as an attic for unused items from the house. Being of thrifty New England stock, the dolls rarely get rid of anything; they simply store it away for possible use later.

The milking stand replicates the one Tasha's goats use twice a day. They stand patiently, munching on pellets or hay, while Tasha milks, often yielding as much as a gallon both morning and evening.

The goats not being milked dine together at what Tasha refers to as the "goat cafeteria." Each goat has her own bucket of food and a single door lifts up, allowing access to everyone's meal at the same time. It is both democratic and practical.

Food for all the animals, including seed for the wild birds, must be laid in before the winter's heavy snows make it impossible to get out to the highway. Grain and pellet storage barrels are everywhere. Tasha is most fond of the large ones, which are hollowed out from single tree trunks. They are solid and heavy and quite rare, but Tasha has been fortunate and persistent enough to collect a number of them, which she uses daily.

Naturally, the dollhouse goat barn had to have one of these hollowed-out barrels, and a miniature version stands filled with an ample supply of food for Emma and Thaddeus's silver Nubian, who occupies the barn and considers it her private domain. Made by Tasha of painted cloth stretched over a wood frame, she was fashioned in the likeness of Severn Silver, one of the first of Tasha's new herd of silver Nubians.

The goats all eat at the same time by virtue of the separated feed buckets. Tasha refers to this arrangement as the GOAT CAFETERIA.

A **PULLEY** outside the loft door is used to pull hay bales up to the loft.

In the early nineteenth century, tree trunks were hollowed out to produce sturdy, **ONE-PIECE BARRELS**. Tasha's barn houses a collection of these unusual barrels, which she cherishes. The dollhouse miniature is an antique and even rarer than the larger ones.

Tools and a prized gourd lend an air of restful industry to the walls of the barn, as they do in Tasha's full-size version. A rope-and-pulley system on the outside wall of the barn makes it easy to hoist bales of hay into the loft. Copies of Tasha's barn windows mounted traditionally high make the most of available light, both in the morning and at twilight.

Christmas

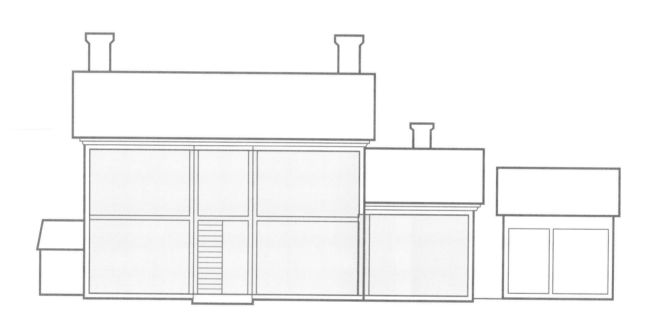

Christmas

CHRISTMAS IN THE DOLLHOUSE closely mirrors Christmas at Corgi Cottage. The tree is similar to Tasha's, with blown-glass ornaments, paper cornucopias filled with sweets, Danish woven-straw ornaments, and paper hearts.

Many of the traditions are the same. Emma hangs an Advent wreath lighted with candles on December 6, as does Tasha. The hanging of the wreath symbolizes the beginning of the Christmas celebration. A carved dove with paper wings is a duplicate of the one Tasha hangs each year, as is the Danish straw decoration hung on the parlor door.

Rare paper doves from Germany, referred to as "dresdens" because of the city of their origin, and garlands of glass beads give an old-world flavor to the tree. The tree fills the parlor, as does the one at Corgi Cottage.

Presents surround the tree, but the dolls' Christmas is calmer now that Tasha's

The **ADVENT WREATH** is always lit on December 6, the birthday of St. Nicholas. Emma's hangs in the center hall, Tasha's in the winter kitchen.

children are grown. When the children were smaller, the dolls' Christmas was a major part of Christmas Eve. The dolls presented the children with activities and gifts to keep them busy while Tasha decorated the large tree and prepared Christmas dinner.

Today, the gifts are only for Emma and Thaddeus, and the elaborate doll dinners are cherished memories. Family traditions and customs change in dollhouses just as they do in real families. Doll-size Christmas cards are still exchanged with friends and fans around the world, and a great many of them are hand painted and cherished for years.

Tiny bisque dolls are among the surprises found in the **PAPER CORNUCOPIAS**, which often contain sweets as well.

Emma, like Tasha, is always in charge of **DECORATING THE TREE**. The placement of the ornaments is traditional. Many seem to know their accustomed places.

The dollhouse tree has tiny kugel **ORNAMENTS**, similar to Tasha's large ones that have been handed down in her family since the 1850s. The pressed paper bird is a German dresden, named for the town of its origin. The Danish straw animals of Tasha's own tree are replicated on the dollhouse tree.

The **CARVED WOODEN BIRD** was fashioned after Tasha's originals, which she carved years ago and hangs each Christmas in her own kitchen window.

The traditional **PLUM PUDDING** is ready to be served at Christmas dinner.

Cookie making remains an ongoing pleasure in the dollhouse, and Emma's skill was featured in a recent video, "Take Peace: A Corgi Cottage Christmas." Originally produced for Tasha's company, Corgi Cottage Industries, the video was subsequently shown on PBS. Emma, like Tasha, makes many boxes of cookies each December for gifts. The kitchen takes on a Christmas feel with miniature Danish straw decorations in the window and fresh evergreens filling the air with their strong crisp scent.

The process of **COOKIE MAKING** is as enjoyable as the result, so Emma never hurries. She carefully rolls out the dough to the desired thickness.

A wire rack allows **TINY COOKIES** to cool before they are wrapped as gifts. Both Emma and Tasha send cookies to friends and other dolls. They are a much-anticipated Christmas present.

Emma and Thaddeus exchange many hand-
painted **CHRISTMAS CARDS** with doll
friends who live all over the world. They
become cherished treasures of friendship.

Thaddeus chooses his GIFTS FOR EMMA
very carefully. It's difficult to find something
for someone who has everything. Most often,
the gifts are handmade.

In a pose reminiscent of
numerous illustrations by Tasha,
EMMA AND THADDEUS are
silhouetted against the backdrop of
their marvelously detailed tree.

THE LIGHTING OF THE TREE is a festive event with
refreshments and toasts.

Christmas in the dollhouse is especially nostalgic, recalling memories of a busy

household filled with children and their friends, of teas and parties for dolls and teddy

bears, and of elaborate marionette shows. It also brings to mind Tasha Tudor's seventh

Christmas, when her mother's gift of a dollhouse inspired Tasha to begin a lifelong tra-

dition of creation in miniature. The beautiful rooms of her dollhouse will depict vividly

for generations to come the world she created and lived in.

Treasures

THE KITCHEN

Commonly known as sugar buckets, **FIRKINS** were widely used in the nineteenth century to store any dry kitchen staple such as grain or flour. Named for a British unit of capacity, miniature firkins are seldom seen.

Emma is as captivated by **BASKETS** as Tasha. Many friends who are skilled basket makers, including Wayne Rundell, have contributed masterful examples to Tasha's and Emma's collections.

Tasha challenged an elderly artisan
to replicate one of her favorite possessions, a handblown, blue-banded
COOKIE JAR, which descended
in her family.

The **SINK** is a replica of Tasha's own. The hand
pump, made by Tasha's brother-in-law, Lauren
McCready, actually works when its reservoir, an
old olive-oil can, is filled with water.

Most of the stoneware pieces in the kitchen are exact copies of Tasha's own crockery, as is this usable cobalt-blue-decorated CHURN, complete with its wooden dasher.

The RED CUPBOARD is a near copy of the large one in Tasha's kitchen. Its open top makes for easy access.

One of Tasha's more recent acquisitions is an
unusual ANTIQUE WOODEN DUSTPAN.
She was so taken with it that her son Seth
created a miniature one for the dollhouse as a
Christmas present for his mother.

Emma's TIN KITCHEN, an exact
replica of Tasha's own, stands ready
to prepare Christmas dinner.

The **PEWTER PORRINGER** is one of the earliest items in the dollhouse, dating from the late eighteenth century. The **TIN-LINED, COPPER DUSTPAN** bears the romantic inscription "My Emma" and was a gift from Thaddeus.

This set of **EVERYDAY FLATWARE** of steel with polished bone handles is stored in an elegantly scalloped wooden cutlery tray.

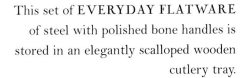

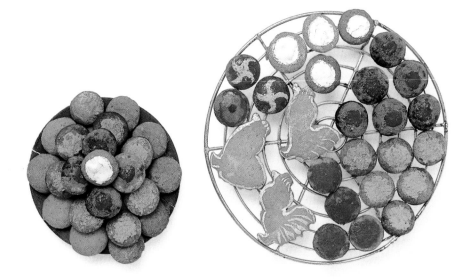

COOKIE MAKING is considered an art at Corgi Cottage as well as in the dollhouse. At Christmas, Emma makes dozens of cookies to send to doll friends. She is careful to save enough for afternoon tea and for festive events such as the lighting of the Advent wreath and the presentation of the tree.

Tasha's cobalt-blue-decorated STONEWARE pottery constitutes an impressive, museum-quality collection, which is frequently seen in her illustrations. Friends who were professional potters made miniature reproductions for the dollhouse kitchen.

THE DINING ROOM

Emma's English blue-and-white CHINA is a floral transfer pattern. The complete set consists of forty pieces.

THE PARLOR

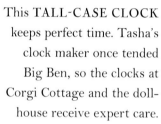

This **TALL-CASE CLOCK** keeps perfect time. Tasha's clock maker once tended Big Ben, so the clocks at Corgi Cottage and the dollhouse receive expert care.

Marjorie Tudor, Tasha's daughter-in-law, made this **CHAIR**, a replica of one of Tasha's. Painstakingly true to the original, Marjorie even duplicated the wear visible on the original.

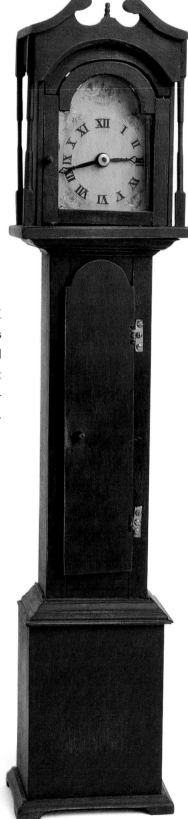

Thaddeus's **MUSKET AND POWDER HORN** are replicas of the ones that hang over the fireplace in Tasha's winter kitchen and that originally belonged to Tasha's great-great-grandfather, William Tudor.

When wound by a key in the shape of a bird, this **BIRD IN A GILDED CAGE** flaps his wings, moves his head, and warbles. The filigree border around the base of the brass cage is jewel-like in its delicacy.

THE CENTER HALL

The dollhouse collection of **AUSTRIAN BRONZES**, remarkable in its own right, has an interesting connection to Beatrix Potter. Many of Potter's characters in bronze were a gift to the dollhouse from her biographer, Leslie Linder. Mr. Tod (the Saxon word for fox), in his green coat, and Benjamin Bunny, wearing a tam, are favorites of Emma and Thaddeus's.

THE BEDROOM

HAND-PAINTED CHRISTMAS CARDS are both sent and received by Emma and Thaddeus, a continuation of the Sparrow Post tradition begun by Tasha, when her children were young, as a form of gracious communication among the children and their dolls and stuffed animals.

The walnut **HIGHBOY**, inspired by an early New England one in Tasha's bathroom, provides storage for clothing used on a daily basis.

Thaddeus's **TOILETRY CASE**, or necessaire, contains all the articles a well-groomed gentleman needs to look his best, including an elegantly gilded safety razor in a case complete with additional razor blades.

The mahogany **BLANKET CHEST** still has its original key. Kept at the foot of Emma and Thaddeus's bed, it provides ample storage for clothing used only on special occasions.

The fading glow of a sunset finds
EMMA in a thoughtful mood.
Her finely detailed blouse is a copy
of one of Tasha's favorites from
her 1830s clothing collection.

THADDEUS relaxes at the end of
a busy day, seemingly reflective in
mood. Behind him on the wall is his
favorite engraving, of ancient ruins.
Thaddeus is rather scholarly in his
taste in art and books.

THE LIBRARY

Emma's art, signed "E.B.," is remarkably Tudor-like in style and subject matter. This **WATERCOLOR** of a bird was sent as a Christmas present to one of Emma's doll friends, Annabelle Greiner. The **OIL PORTRAIT OF EMMA** was painted in Paris and presented to her as a gift.

Emma's **SCRAPBOOK** is authentic and exceedingly rare in such a small size. It is filled with real Victorian "scraps," tiny embossed pictures of people, animals, birds, flowers, fruit, humorous situations, and virtually everything eclectic that Victorians were interested in. Victorians collected the scraps in books, and consequently gave the name to a broader use of any blank book containing personal memorabilia.

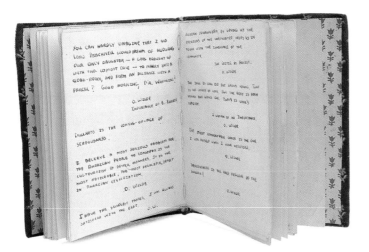

The keeping of a **COMMONPLACE BOOK** containing favorite quotations was considered necessary for people who wished to be prepared for polite conversation in society. Emma's commonplace book contains 125 quotations that show the broad range of her interests. Favorites are from Thoreau, Emerson, and Oscar Wilde. Coincidentally, they are Tasha's favorites as well.

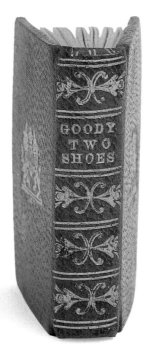

Many of the volumes in Emma and Thaddeus's library are handsomely bound in leather with detailed gold tooling. This **THREE-VOLUME SET OF HERALDRY** contains many full-color coats of arms.

An exquisitely **BOUND EDITION** of *The History of Little Goody Two-Shoes* is typical of the library's collection of nineteenth-century instruction-by-example stories for children.

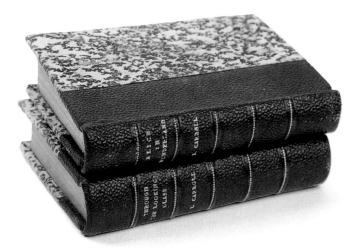

Fine hand-tooled LEATHER BINDINGS abound in Tasha's and the dollhouse libraries. *Abraham Lincoln* and *From a Writer's Notebook* were both published by Achille St. Onge, who also produced slightly larger leather-bound editions of Tasha's *The Night Before Christmas* and *The Twenty-Third Psalm.* *Alice in Wonderland* and *Through the Looking Glass* are particular favorites. One photograph album contains only photographs of dolls; the other, photographs of their owners.

These INSTRUMENTS are part of the eight-piece set made for Thaddeus by miniaturist Harry Smith and are excellent examples of the accurate detail for which he is famous. The instruments are loaned to the Corgi Orchestra for performances.

This working **SPINNING WHEEL** is a copy of one of Tasha's numerous wheels. Made by the renowned miniaturist Harry Smith, it retains all the delicacy and efficiency of the original.

THE GOAT BARN

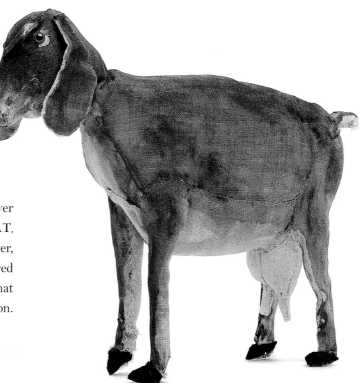

Tasha made this silver **NUBIAN GOAT**, named Severn Silver, shortly after she acquired her first goat with that distinctive coloration.

Biography

TASHA TUDOR was born in Boston in 1915 to parents who imparted to her the value and joy of being individual and original. Her mother was the portraitist Rosamond Tudor and her father the noted naval architect William Starling Burgess. Both sides of Tasha's family had been prominent in Boston for generations. Their circle of friends included Emerson, the Alcotts, Thoreau, Mark Twain, Oliver Wendell Holmes Jr., Albert Einstein, and Buckminster Fuller.

From an early age, Tasha felt that she had once lived in the 1830s. Her knowledge of that period was instinctive and flawless. Even before she was a teenager, she began to make her own clothes following only the patterns in her head. They turned out to be exact copies of clothing popular a century earlier. From the age of seven, she also knew she wanted to be an artist and she practiced her craft relentlessly.

Tasha surrounded herself with things from the 1830s and painted the life she was living. From the beginning, her art and her life were interchangeable and she established a pattern she would follow for the next three-quarters of a century.

Tasha's first book, *Pumpkin Moonshine*, was originally turned down by every publisher in New York. Realizing that the publishing houses had seen only the original art and manuscript but not her version of what the complete book should look like, Tasha remained undaunted. She sewed a tiny volume together with a handmade calico cover and vowed to make the rounds of publishers again. This time, she succeeded on her first try. Published in 1938, *Pumpkin Moonshine* quickly became an American classic and four more calico books followed.

She used her royalties to buy a farm in New Hampshire and completely immersed herself in an 1830s lifestyle while raising four children in an original and independent manner.

As the decades passed, Tasha continued to be consistently prolific and popular. Her edition of *The Secret Garden* sold an amazing two million copies, making it one of the bestselling children's books of all time.

Tasha has written, illustrated, or been the subject of more than eighty-seven books. Firmly ensconced in the pantheon of the most prolific and revered illustrators, Tasha has in recent years, with the publication of *The Private World of Tasha Tudor, Tasha Tudor's Cookbook, Tasha Tudor's Garden,* and *Tasha Tudor's Heirloom Crafts,* become equally well known for her lifestyle.

Tasha has accumulated an impressive list of awards and honors during a lifetime of illustrating some of the twentieth century's most popular children's books. She has won Caldecott honors twice, as well as the Regina Medal.

The honor closest to her heart came in 1996 when the Abby Aldrich Rockefeller Folk Art Center, in Williamsburg, Virginia, mounted a major exhibition focusing not only on Tasha's art but also on the lifestyle that nurtured the art. In describing the exhibition, the Colonial Williamsburg Foundation stated: "For sixty years her work has filled storybooks, now it's filling a museum." The exhibition, "Take Joy! The Magical World of Tasha Tudor," was unprecedented in scope, content, and participation by a living artist and attracted record-breaking crowds. It firmly established Tasha's legacy in a manner rarely afforded an artist still at her creative and productive best.

Bibliography

*Titles are arranged chronologically
by date of publication.*

Pumpkin Moonshine. Written and illustrated by Tasha Tudor. New York: Oxford University Press, 1938.

Alexander the Gander. Written and illustrated by Tasha Tudor. New York: Oxford University Press, 1939.

The County Fair. Written and illustrated by Tasha Tudor. New York: Oxford University Press, 1940.

Snow Before Christmas. Written and illustrated by Tasha Tudor. New York: Oxford University Press, 1941.

A Tale for Easter. Written and illustrated by Tasha Tudor. New York: Oxford University Press, 1941.

Dorcas Porkus. Written and illustrated by Tasha Tudor. New York: Oxford University Press, 1942.

The White Goose. Written and illustrated by Tasha Tudor. New York: Oxford University Press, 1943.

Mother Goose. Illustrated by Tasha Tudor. New York: Oxford University Press, 1944.

Fairy Tales from Hans Christian Andersen by Hans Christian Andersen. Illustrated by Tasha Tudor. New York: Oxford University Press, 1945.

Linsey Woolsey. Written and illustrated by Tasha Tudor. New York: Oxford University Press, 1946.

A Child's Garden of Verses by Robert Louis Stevenson. Illustrated by Tasha Tudor. New York: Oxford University Press, 1947.

Jackanapes by Juliet Ewing. Illustrated by Tasha Tudor. New York: Oxford University Press, 1948.

Thistly B. Written and illustrated by Tasha Tudor. New York: Oxford University Press, 1949.

The Dolls' Christmas. Written and illustrated by Tasha Tudor. New York: Oxford University Press, 1950.

Amanda and the Bear. Written and illustrated by Tasha Tudor. New York: Oxford University Press, 1951.

First Prayers. Illustrated by Tasha Tudor. New York: Oxford University Press, 1952.

Edgar Allen Crow. Written and illustrated by Tasha Tudor. New York: Oxford University Press, 1953.

A Is for Annabelle. Written and illustrated by Tasha Tudor. New York: Oxford University Press, 1954.

Biggety Bantam by T. L. McCready Jr. Illustrated by Tasha Tudor. New York: Ariel, 1954.

First Graces. Illustrated by Tasha Tudor. New York: Oxford University Press, 1955.

Pekin White by T. L. McCready Jr. Illustrated by Tasha Tudor. New York: Ariel, 1955.

Mr. Stubbs by T. L. McCready Jr. Illustrated by Tasha Tudor. New York: Ariel, 1956.

1 Is One. Written and illustrated by Tasha Tudor. New York: Oxford University Press, 1956.

Around the Year. Written and illustrated by Tasha Tudor. New York: Oxford University Press, 1957.

And It Was So. Illustrated by Tasha Tudor. Philadelphia: Westminster Press, 1958.

Increase Rabbit by T. L. McCready Jr. Illustrated by Tasha Tudor. New York: Ariel, 1958.

Adventures of a Beagle by T. L. McCready Jr. Illustrated by Tasha Tudor. New York: Ariel, 1959.

The Lord Will Love Thee. Illustrated by Tasha Tudor. Philadelphia: Westminster Press, 1959.

Becky's Birthday. Written and illustrated by Tasha Tudor. New York: Viking, 1960.

My Brimful Book. Illustrated by Tasha Tudor, Margot Austin, and Wesley Dennis. New York: Platt & Munk, 1960.

Becky's Christmas. Written and illustrated by Tasha Tudor. New York: Viking, 1961.

The Tasha Tudor Book of Fairy Tales. Illustrated by Tasha Tudor. New York: Platt & Munk, 1961.

The Dolls' House by Rumer Godden. Illustrated by Tasha Tudor. New York: Viking, 1962.

The Night Before Christmas by Clement C. Moore. Illustrated by Tasha Tudor. Worcester, Mass.: St. Onge, 1962.

The Secret Garden by Frances Hodgson Burnett. Illustrated by Tasha Tudor. Philadelphia: Lippincott, 1962.

A Little Princess by Frances Hodgson Burnett. Illustrated by Tasha Tudor. Philadelphia: Lippincott, 1963.

A Round Dozen by Louisa May Alcott. Illustrated by Tasha Tudor. New York: Viking, 1963.

Wings from the Wind. Illustrated by Tasha Tudor. Philadelphia: Lippincott, 1964.

Tasha Tudor's Favorite Stories. Illustrated by Tasha Tudor. Philadelphia: Lippincott, 1965.

The Twenty-Third Psalm. Illustrated by Tasha Tudor. Worcester, Mass.: St. Onge, 1965.

First Delights. Illustrated by Tasha Tudor. New York: Platt & Munk, 1966.

Take Joy! The Tasha Tudor Christmas Book. Selected, edited, and illustrated by Tasha Tudor. New York: World, 1966.

Wind in the Willows by Kenneth Grahame. Illustrated by Tasha Tudor. New York: World, 1966.

First Poems of Childhood. Illustrated by Tasha Tudor. New York: Platt & Munk, 1967.

More Prayers. Illustrated by Tasha Tudor. New York: Henry Z. Walck, 1967.

The Real Diary of a Real Boy by Henry A. Shute. Illustrated by Tasha Tudor. Peterborough, N.H.: Noone House, 1967.

Brite and Fair by Henry A. Shute. Illustrated by Tasha Tudor. Peterborough, N.H.: Noone House, 1968.

The New England Butt'ry Shelf Cookbook by Mary Campbell. Illustrated by Tasha Tudor. New York: World, 1968.

Little Women by Louisa May Alcott. Illustrated by Tasha Tudor. New York: World, 1968.

The New England Butt'ry Shelf Almanac by Mary Campbell. Illustrated by Tasha Tudor. New York: World, 1970.

Betty Crocker's Kitchen Gardens by Mary Campbell. Illustrated by Tasha Tudor. New York: Universal Publishing, 1971.

Corgiville Fair. Written and illustrated by Tasha Tudor. New York: Thomas Y. Crowell, 1971.

The Night Before Christmas by Clement C. Moore. Illustrated by Tasha Tudor. Chicago: Rand McNally, 1975.

The Christmas Cat by Efner Tudor Holmes. Illustrated by Tasha Tudor. New York: Thomas Y. Crowell, 1976.

Amy's Goose by Efner Tudor Holmes. Illustrated by Tasha Tudor. New York: Thomas Y. Crowell, 1977.

A Time to Keep. Written and illustrated by Tasha Tudor. Chicago: Rand McNally, 1977.

The Tasha Tudor Bedtime Book. Illustrated by Tasha Tudor. New York: Platt & Munk, 1977.

Tasha Tudor's Sampler. Written and illustrated by Tasha Tudor. New York: David McKay, 1977.

Carrie's Gift by Efner Tudor Holmes. Illustrated by Tasha Tudor. New York: Collins & World, 1978.

Tasha Tudor's Favorite Christmas Carols. Illustrated by Tasha Tudor and Linda Allen. New York: David McKay, 1978.

Tasha Tudor's Five Senses. Written and illustrated by Tasha Tudor. New York: Platt & Munk, 1978.

Tasha Tudor's Old-Fashioned Gifts. Written and illustrated by Tasha Tudor and Linda Allen. New York: David McKay, 1979.

Drawn From New England by Bethany Tudor. Illustrated by Tasha Tudor. New York: Collins & World, 1979.

A Book of Christmas. Written and illustrated by Tasha Tudor. New York: Collins & World, 1979.

Springs of Joy. Illustrated by Tasha Tudor. Chicago: Rand McNally, 1979.

The Lord Is My Shepherd. Illustrated by Tasha Tudor. New York: Philomel, 1980.

The Illustrated Treasury of Humor for Children. Illustrated by Tasha Tudor and others. New York: Grosset and Dunlap, 1980.

Rosemary for Remembrance. Written and illustrated by Tasha Tudor. New York: Philomel, 1981.

A Child's Garden of Verses by Robert Louis Stevenson. Illustrated by Tasha Tudor. Chicago: Rand McNally, 1981.

The Platt & Munk Treasury of Stories for Children. Illustrated by Tasha Tudor and others. New York: Platt & Munk, 1981.

Tasha Tudor's Treasures. Illustrated by Tasha Tudor. New York: Henry Z. Walck, 1982.

A Basket of Herbs. Illustrated by Tasha Tudor. Brattleboro, Vt.: Stephen Green, 1983.

All for Love. Illustrated by Tasha Tudor. New York: Philomel, 1984.

Seasons of Delight. A Year on an Old-Fashioned Farm. Written and illustrated by Tasha Tudor. New York: Philomel, 1986.

Give Us This Day. Illustrated by Tasha Tudor. New York: Philomel, 1987.

Tasha Tudor's Advent Calendar. Written and illustrated by Tasha Tudor. New York: Philomel, 1988.

Tasha Tudor Sketchbook. Written and illustrated by Tasha Tudor. Mooresville, Ind.: Jenny Wren Press, 1989.

Tasha Tudor Miniature Gift Set. Illustrated by Tasha Tudor. New York: Philomel, 1989.

A Brighter Garden. Selected poems by Emily Dickinson. Illustrated by Tasha Tudor. New York: Philomel, 1990.

The Real Pretend by Joan Donaldson. Illustrated by Tasha Tudor. New York: Checkerboard Press, 1992.

The Private World of Tasha Tudor. Written and illustrated by Tasha Tudor. Photographs by Richard Brown. Boston: Little, Brown and Company, 1992.

Tasha Tudor's Cookbook. Written and illustrated by Tasha Tudor. Boston: Little, Brown and Company, 1993.

Tasha Tudor's Garden by Tovah Martin. Illustrated by Tasha Tudor. Photographs by Richard Brown. Boston: Houghton Mifflin, 1994.

Tasha Tudor's Heirloom Crafts by Tovah Martin. Illustrated by Tasha Tudor. Photographs by Richard Brown. Boston: Houghton Mifflin, 1995.

The Tasha Tudor Sketchbook Series: Family and Friends. Written and illustrated by Tasha Tudor. Richmond, Va.: Corgi Cottage Industries, 1995.

The Great Corgiville Kidnapping. Written and illustrated by Tasha Tudor. Boston: Little, Brown and Company, 1997.

The Night Before Christmas by Clement C. Moore. Illustrated by Tasha Tudor. Boston: Little, Brown and Company, 1999.